# love your
## leftovers

# love your leftovers

### FEED YOUR FRIENDS & FAMILY FOR NEXT TO NOTHING

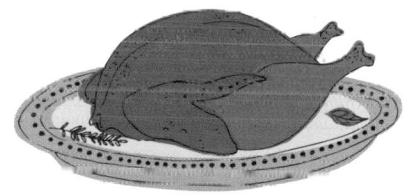

## CICO BOOKS
LONDON NEW YORK

Published in 2009 by CICO Books
an imprint of Ryland Peters & Small Ltd
20–21 Jockey's Fields, London WC1R 4BW

www.cicobooks.co.uk

10 9 8 7 6 5 4 3 2 1

A CIP catalogue record for this book is
available from the British Library.

ISBN-13: 978 1 906525 84 2

Printed in China

Editor: Gillian Haslam
Designer: Paul Tilby
Illustrator: Trina Dalziel

# contents

4 tablespoons extra virgin olive or sunflower oil

3 medium potatoes, about 325 g, peeled and cubed

1 onion, halved and sliced

75 g green beans, trimmed and cut into 3

4 asparagus spears, cut into 5-cm lengths

1 red pepper, quartered, deseeded and thinly sliced

75 g spicy chorizo, sliced

1 garlic clove, finely chopped

6 large eggs

75 g frozen peas

sea salt and freshly ground black pepper

**SERVES 4–6**

## hearty country-style tortilla

*A robust omelette packed full of goodness, this is a perfect recipe for using up small quantities of leftover vegetables, including ingredients such as broccoli, corn, broad beans or mushrooms. This tortilla is best finished under the grill to retain the lovely colours on the top when serving.*

Preheat the grill to medium.

Heat 2 tablespoons of the oil in a large, heavy based non-stick frying pan. Add the potatoes and cook over a medium heat for 5 minutes. Add the onion and cook for 10 minutes or until the potatoes are almost tender, lifting and turning occasionally.

Meanwhile, put the beans and asparagus in a saucepan of salted boiling water and cook for 5 minutes. Drain and refresh in cold water. Drain well.

Add the pepper, chorizo, asparagus, beans and garlic to the potatoes and cook for 5 minutes, stirring frequently.

Break the eggs into a large bowl, season and whisk briefly with a fork. Mix in the peas and cooked vegetable mixture.

If necessary, wipe out the frying pan with kitchen paper, then add the remaining oil and heat until hot. Add the tortilla mixture, letting it spread evenly in the pan.

Cook over a medium-low heat for about 10 minutes until the bottom is golden brown and the top almost set. Slide under the preheated grill to set and lightly brown the top. Transfer to a serving plate, cut into wedges and serve hot or warm.

# carbonara

Brilliant for a quick after-work supper and a great way to use up hard cheese and leftover cream, this dish is ready to eat in the time it takes the pasta to cook. It's traditionally served with spaghetti, but any long or ribbon shape, such as tagliatelle or linguine, will be fine.

Bring a large saucepan of water to the boil. Add a good pinch of salt, then the pasta, and cook until al dente, or according to the timings on the packet.

Meanwhile, heat the butter in a small frying pan, add the onion or shallot, garlic and bacon and cook for 5 minutes until golden. Put the eggs, cream and cheese into a bowl and beat, adding salt and pepper to taste.

Drain the pasta and return it to the warm pan. Remove from the heat and add the shallot mixture. Add the egg mixture and toss well to coat. Divide between 2 serving bowls, sprinkle with Parmesan and black pepper, then serve.

Variation: Alfredo sauce is very similar to Carbonara but even simpler. Toss hot cooked pasta (traditionally linguine) with double cream, butter and grated Parmesan, sprinkle with black pepper and serve.

200 g dried pasta, such as spaghetti or linguine

1 tablespoon butter

1/4 onion or 1 shallot, finely chopped

2 garlic cloves, finely chopped

6 slices smoked streaky bacon, chopped

2 eggs

150 ml single cream

2 tablespoons freshly grated Parmesan or Cheddar cheese, plus extra to serve

salt and freshly ground black pepper

**SERVES 2**

# rarebit

25 g butter

1 onion, sliced

100 g Cheddar or Gruyère cheese, grated

75 ml ale or lager

1 teaspoon mustard

2 eggs, lightly beaten

4 slices of bread

a pinch of sea salt and freshly ground black pepper

**SERVES 2–4**

'Welsh rabbit' – also known as rarebit – is a glorified version of cheese on toast. It dates back to the mid-sixteenth century and has evolved into countless variations. This easy-to-make rarebit is hard to beat as a comforting snack or light brunch and the perfect way to use cheese that has turned hard.

Melt the butter in a heavy-based saucepan, add the onion and cook until softened. Add the cheese, ale, mustard and salt. Stir over low heat until the cheese has melted.

Add the beaten eggs and stir until the mixture has thickened slightly, about 2–3 minutes. Don't overcook it or you will end up with scrambled eggs.

Meanwhile, toast the bread on both sides, then spoon the cheese mixture onto the toast and cook under a hot grill until puffed and gold-flecked. Serve with lots of black pepper.

## cheese scones

Savoury scones filled with cream cheese and
salad, or topped with sweet juicy grapes,
make a wonderful afternoon snack. They are
just a few mouthfuls each, so you'll still have
plenty of room for a few cakes and fancies.
Hard cheese is ideal for grating, and these
scones could also be frozen.

Preheat the oven to 220°C (425°C) Gas 7.

Put the flour, baking powder, salt and pepper in a food processor and pulse to combine.
Add the butter and process for about 20 seconds until the mixture resembles fine
breadcrumbs. Transfer to a large bowl and stir in 50 g of the cheese, then make a well
in the centre of the mixture.

Beat together the egg and milk in another bowl, reserving 1 tablespoon of the mixture
in a separate bowl. Pour most of the remaining liquid into the flour mixture and bring
together into a soft dough using a fork. If there are still dry crumbs, add a little more
of the liquid. Turn out onto a lightly floured surface and knead very briefly, then gently
pat or roll out to about 2 cm thick. Cut out rounds with a 4-cm biscuit cutter, pressing
the trimmings together to make more scones.

Arrange the scones on a greased baking sheet, spacing them slightly apart. Brush the
tops with the reserved egg and milk mixture and sprinkle over the remaining cheese.
Bake for about 10 minutes, or until risen and golden. Transfer to a wire rack and leave
to cool.

To serve, split the scones and spread the bottom half with a thick layer of cream
cheese, top with salad, then finish with the scone lid. Alternatively, split the scones,
spread each half with cream cheese and top with halved grapes.

225 g plain flour

4 teaspoons baking powder

a pinch of salt

$1/4$ teaspoon freshly ground
black pepper

50 g unsalted butter,
chilled and cubed

75 g mature Cheddar
cheese, grated

1 egg

100 ml milk

### to serve

about 150 g cream cheese

about 40 g lettuce, cucumber or
200 g seedless grapes, halved

**MAKES 16 SCONES**

# cheese pasta bake

350 g dried pasta, such as penne

400 g cream cheese

2 tablespoons wholegrain mustard

300 g hard cheese, grated

4 tablespoons freshly grated
Parmesan cheese

salt and freshly ground black
pepper

**SERVES 4**

This is a simplified version of that old-time favourite, macaroni cheese, but with no flour and no risk of lumps in the sauce. You can use any shape of pasta and whatever hard cheese you have that needs to be eaten up.

Preheat the oven to 200°C (400°F) Gas 6. Bring a large saucepan of water to the boil. Add a good pinch of salt, then the pasta, and cook until al dente, or according to the timings on the packet. Drain the pasta well and return it to the warm pan.

Add the cream cheese and stir to mix. Add the mustard, hard cheese and Parmesan, season with salt and pepper to taste. Stir to mix.

Transfer to a baking dish and bake for 25–30 minutes until golden and bubbling.

# yoghurt cake

This is such a simple cake that there's no excuse not to serve it up for dessert. The yoghurt pot is the measure, so it doesn't really matter what size you use. Plain, French-style set yoghurt works well. If you don't fancy orange, try other flavourings: cinnamon, honey, vanilla, chocolate, fruit pieces, etc. This is great to make, and eat, with children, and the perfect way to use up a pot of yoghurt approaching its use-by date.

Preheat the oven to 180°C (350°F) Gas 4. Grease a deep, 23-cm diameter cake tin.

Empty the yoghurt into a large bowl and wipe out the pot so when you measure the other ingredients, they won't stick. Add the sugar, flour, eggs, oil, bicarbonate of soda, salt and half the orange juice. Stir well.

Pour into the prepared cake tin and bake in the preheated oven until a knife inserted in the middle comes out clean, about 15–20 minutes.

Remove from the oven and pierce a few holes in the top with a fork. Pour over the remaining orange juice. Leave to cool slightly, then turn out onto a wire rack to cool. Dust with icing sugar and serve at room temperature.

a pot of natural set yoghurt
2 pots of sugar
3 pots of flour
2 eggs
1 tablespoon sunflower oil
1 teaspoon bicarbonate of soda
a pinch of salt
freshly squeezed juice of 1 orange
1 tablespoon icing sugar,
to decorate

**SERVES 8**

# american pancakes

A stack of fluffy, American-style pancakes in the morning will keep you fuelled for hours. Make the batter before bedtime and leave it overnight in the fridge. In the morning, you'll have a brunch feast in minutes. Great if you have weekend guests.

250 g plain flour
2 teaspoons baking powder
1 teaspoon sea salt
3 tablespoons sugar
250 ml milk
2 eggs, lightly beaten
50 g unsalted butter, melted, plus extra for cooking

**maple butter syrup**

80 ml maple syrup
25 g unsalted butter

**MAKES 8–12**

Sift the flour, baking powder, salt and sugar into a bowl. Mix the milk, eggs and melted butter in a large jug, then add the flour mixture and mix quickly to make a batter (don't worry about lumps – they're good!). Alternatively, make the batter in a bowl and transfer to a jug.

Heat a cast-iron frying pan or flat-surfaced griddle until medium hot. Grease lightly with extra butter, then pour in the batter in batches to make rounds 8–10 cm in diameter. Cook for 1–2 minutes or until bubbles form on top of the pancakes and the underside is golden, then flip each one over and cook for 1 minute more. Keep the pancakes warm on a plate in a low oven while you cook the remaining batches.

Gently heat the maple syrup and butter together in a small saucepan or in a heatproof bowl in the microwave until the butter is melted. Stack the pancakes on warmed plates and pour over the buttery syrup.

3 egg whites
175 g caster sugar
$^1/_4$ teaspoon ground cardamom
200 ml double cream
1 tablespoon clear honey
1 tablespoon rosewater
pomegranate seeds, to serve
(optional)

**SERVES 6**

# meringues
## with rosewater cream

These light-as-air meringues are particularly good served with fresh pomegranate seeds, but work equally well with other fruits such as cherries, nectarines or peaches. Meringues are a good way to use up egg whites, leftover when the yolks have been used in another recipe. Instead of rosewater cream, you could also top the meringues with whipped cream and fresh fruit.

Preheat the oven to 160°C (325°F) Gas 3. Line a baking tray with baking parchment.

Put the egg whites in a grease-free bowl and whisk until they start to peak. Gradually whisk in the sugar, a spoonful at a time, until the mixture becomes very thick and glossy. Gently fold in the ground cardamom.

Drop 12 spoonfuls of the meringue mixture onto the prepared baking tray, leaving a gap between each mound. Bake in the preheated oven for 1 hour. Remove from the oven, transfer the meringues to a wire rack and let cool.

Put the cream, honey and rosewater into a bowl and whip until the mixture just holds its shape. Put a couple of spoonfuls of the whipped cream into each of six serving bowls, add two meringues to each one and top with the pomegranate seeds, if using.

# 2 lovely old veg

## pumpkin risotto

500 g peeled and deseeded pumpkin or butternut squash

4 potatoes, peeled and cut into large chunks (optional)

2 tablespoons butter

milk (optional – see method)

4 tablespoons olive oil

2 onions, finely chopped

2 fat garlic cloves, crushed

400 g risotto rice, such as arborio or carnaroli

1 litre boiling chicken stock

salt

**to serve**

your choice of:

shavings of Parmesan cheese

pumpkin crisps

herbs

**SERVES 4**

Pumpkin is a delicious but huge vegetable, so there is usually a lot leftover – here's a great way to make the most of it. And if you carve pumpkins at Halloween, save the flesh for this risotto. The potatoes are optional, but if you use a butternut squash, they will help compensate for its looser texture.

Put the pumpkin and potatoes in a saucepan, barely cover with water, add salt and simmer until the vegetables are tender. Drain, reserving the cooking water. Purée the pumpkin and potatoes with half the butter (a hand-held blender is useful here), and add enough of the cooking water to make a thick, soupy mixture – add a little milk if necessary. Keep the mixture hot.

Heat the oil and remaining butter in a frying pan, add the onions and sauté gently until soft and translucent. Add the garlic and cook until lightly golden, about 1–2 minutes. Add the rice and stir-fry for 1–2 minutes until the grains are well-covered with oil. Add a quarter of the boiling stock and simmer gently, stirring, until absorbed.

Repeat until all the stock has been used and the risotto is creamy and fluffy, about 18–20 minutes. Stir the reserved pumpkin purée through the risotto and serve, topped with the Parmesan, pumpkin crisps and herbs, if using.

500 g medium or baby courgettes
3 tablespoons olive oil
1 mozzarella cheese
cherry or mini plum tomatoes
salt and freshly ground black
pepper
4 slices of bread, toasted

**parsley oil**

a large bunch of parsley, with stalks
250 ml extra virgin olive oil
a pinch of salt

**SERVES 4**

# grilled courgettes
## with parsley oil

If you grow your own courgettes, you'll often be faced with a glut of them in summer, so here's a great way to serve them. Try a mixture of green and yellow courgettes and use on bruschetta, as an antipasto, as a salad, or with meat, fish or poultry. The parsley oil is optional, but it's a tasty way to use up a big bunch of this fresh herb.

To make the parsley oil, coarsely chop the parsley, then place in a food processor and chop for about 30 seconds. Gradually add the olive oil and keep working to form a green purée. Add a pinch of salt and purée again. Set aside, preferably overnight in the refrigerator, but for at least 30 minutes, to develop flavour and colour. Strain through a fine nylon sieve into a jug or bowl and use for this and other recipes.

To cook the courgettes, cut them lengthways into 5 mm slices. Put in a plastic bag, add the olive oil, salt and pepper and shake to coat. Heat a stove-top grill pan over medium heat until hot, add the courgette slices and cook for about 2 minutes on each side until barred with brown and cooked through but not wilted.

Cut the tomatoes in half and pull the mozzarella cheese into shreds. Arrange the courgettes on the toasted bruschetta with the tomatoes and mozzarella pieces. Drizzle with parsley oil, sprinkle with salt and pepper and serve.

# pepper omelette

An omelette should be cooked slowly and be only lightly coloured and still slightly moist when served. The Italians usually flip them to finish cooking, but often a recipe will suggest quickly flashing the omelette under the grill or putting it in a hot oven just to set the top. They can also be cut into squares and served cold, if desired. Use any combinations of peppers in this dish – whatever you have that needs eating up!

Put the peppers skin side up under a preheated grill and cook until the skins have charred. Transfer to a bowl, cover and let cool. This will steam off the skins, making them easier to remove.

Put the cheese in a large bowl, add 1 egg and mix to loosen the cheese. Whisk in the remaining eggs with a fork. Season with salt, pepper and thyme and stir into the cheese mixture.

Peel the charred skins off the peppers and rinse under cold running water. Pat dry with kitchen paper and cut into thick strips. Stir into the bowl.

Heat half the oil in a large, heavy-based frying pan, add the sliced onion and balsamic vinegar and cook over gentle heat for about 10 minutes until softened. Add the garlic and cook for 1 minute.

Using a slotted spoon, add the onion to the egg mixture and stir. Add the remaining oil to the pan and heat gently. Pour the omelette mixture into the pan and let cook over low heat until almost set, puffy and light golden-brown on the underside.

Finish under a preheated grill or put a plate or flat saucepan lid on top of the pan and invert the pan so the omelette drops onto the plate or lid. Slide back into the pan and cook for 30–60 seconds. Transfer to a serving plate and serve hot or at room temperature, cut into wedges.

1 small red pepper, quartered and deseeded

1 small yellow pepper, quartered and deseeded

1 small green pepper, quartered and deseeded

2 tablespoons ricotta or mascarpone cheese

6 large eggs

2 tablespoons fresh thyme leaves

2 tablespoons extra virgin olive or sunflower oil

1 large red onion, sliced

1 tablespoon balsamic vinegar

2 garlic cloves, crushed

salt and freshly ground black pepper

**SERVES 2–3**

## chickpea & vegetable curry

1½ tablespoons vegetable oil
1 garlic clove, crushed
1 red onion, chopped
2 cm ginger, peeled and finely chopped
1½ teaspoons curry powder
1 teaspoon ground coriander
¼ teaspoon fenugreek
¼ teaspoon crushed dried chillies
200 g canned chopped tomatoes
400 g potatoes, cut into 2.5 cm pieces
½ cauliflower, cut into florets
400 g canned chickpeas, drained and rinsed
250 g spinach, chopped
120 g okra, halved lengthways

**to serve**

naan bread
poppadoms

**SERVES 6**

This curry is very simple to make and you can change any of the vegetables to suit whatever you have available. As with all curries, this one can be made in advance and left overnight for the flavours to deepen and intensify.

Heat the oil in a large saucepan, add the garlic, onion and ginger and cook over low heat for 10 minutes until softened. Add the curry powder, coriander, fenugreek and dried chillies, mix well and cook for a further 4 minutes.

Add the tomatoes and 50 ml water, then add the potatoes, cauliflower and chickpeas. Mix well and simmer for about 15 minutes, stirring frequently.

Add the spinach and okra, mix well and simmer for a further 5 minutes. You may need to add a little extra water at this final stage. Serve with naan bread and poppadoms.

## tomato & bean soup

500 ml crushed tomatoes
500 g cooked red kidney beans
500 ml chicken stock
2 garlic cloves, crushed
juice of 1 large lemon
2 tablespoons harissa paste
or chilli paste
salt

**SERVES 4–6**

A very quick and comforting soup – a food processor will give a coarser, more interesting texture than a blender. This is the perfect way to use tomatoes that are over-ripe.

Put the tomatoes, beans and stock in a food processor, in batches if necessary, and pulse briefly until coarsely chopped but not smooth. Transfer to a saucepan, add the crushed garlic, lemon juice and harissa paste and heat to just below boiling, stirring. Thin with boiling water, if necessary. Season, then serve.

Variation: Serve sprinkled with chopped parsley, snipped chives, grated Parmesan cheese and crusty bread on the side.

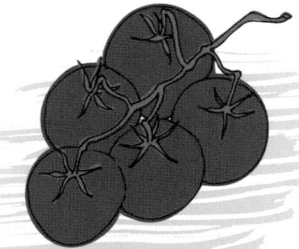

# roasted vegetables

This dish of mixed vegetables roasted to sweetness is deceptively simple. Its success depends on good olive oil and vegetables cooked in their skins for extra flavour. As well as the vegetables suggested here, you could add baby new potatoes in their skins, cherry tomatoes, chunks of sweet potato or courgette, parsnips – in fact, almost anything from your vegetable box. Just bear in mind that some 'hard' vegetables, such as potatoes, take longer to cook, so cut them into smaller chunks. Serve as either an accompaniment or a main dish with bread.

Preheat the oven to 250°C (475°F) Gas 9.

Leave the stems on the peppers, but remove and discard the pith and seeds. Cut the onions almost in half crossways, leaving one side joined, as a hinge. Remove and discard the seeds and pith from the squash but leave otherwise intact.

Cut the unpeeled heads of garlic almost in half crossways, leaving a hinge of papery skin. Pour a teaspoon of the olive oil over the cut surfaces of the garlic, then put the bulbs back together again. Wrap up in foil, to make 2 packets.

Arrange all the prepared vegetables, including the aubergines, in a single layer in 1 or 2 roasting tins, cut sides uppermost. Sprinkle with 3–4 tablespoons of the oil.

Roast in the oven for 35–40 minutes or until soft and fragrant. Transfer to a serving dish and sprinkle with black pepper and the herbs and remaining oil. Serve hot or warm.

2 red peppers, halved lengthways

2 yellow or orange peppers, halved lengthways

2 red onions, unpeeled

4 slices butternut squash or pumpkin, about 1.5 cm thick, deseeded if necessary, or 2 large courgettes, halved lengthways, scored with a fork

2 baby aubergines or 1 large, sliced lengthways and scored with a fork

2 whole garlic heads

6–8 tablespoons olive oil

freshly ground black pepper

1 small handful of fresh herbs, such as parsley, oregano, mint and thyme

**SERVES 4**

# cauliflower cheese

A regular accompaniment on many menus, this recipe is a great way to use up florets of cauliflower and cheese that has become slightly too hard. The secret is to blanch it first, and if you parboil it with a bay leaf the unpleasant cabbage aroma disappears.

1 large cauliflower, separated into large florets
1 fresh bay leaf
500 ml double cream
1 egg
2 teaspoons Dijon mustard
160 g finely grated cheese
salt

**SERVES 4–6**

Preheat the oven to 200°C (400°F) Gas 6. Grease a baking dish.

Bring a large saucepan of water to the boil, add the bay leaf, salt generously, then add the cauliflower. Cook until still slightly firm, about 10 minutes. Drain and set aside.

Put the cream in a saucepan and bring to the boil. Boil for 10 minutes, then stir in the mustard, the egg and 1 teaspoon salt.

Divide the cauliflower into smaller florets, then stir into the cream sauce. Transfer to the prepared baking dish and sprinkle the cheese over the top in an even layer. Bake in the preheated oven until golden, about 40–45 minutes. Serve hot as a side dish or a light supper.

# carrot & spinach mash

This is a flavoursome, yet simple alternative to boiled carrots. Sweet and buttery, it is perfect comfort food. If you buy packets of spinach from the supermarket, you'll find that it doesn't last very long, even if stored in the fridge, so rather than eating steamed spinach two days in a row, try this recipe instead.

400 g carrots, peeled
and chopped
75 g butter
300 g spinach, chopped
sea salt and freshly ground black
pepper

**SERVES 8**

Cook the carrots in a saucepan of lightly salted boiling water for 20 minutes, or until tender. Drain well.

Return the carrots to the pan and put over low heat. Steam off the excess water, stirring frequently, for 2 minutes.

Remove the pan from the heat, add the butter, salt and pepper and mash the carrots well. Add the spinach to the mash and stir for 2 minutes, until wilted. Serve immediately.

# pappa al pomodoro

This is just one of those dishes that, once tasted, is never forgotten. Pappa al pomodoro is a Tuscan 'soup', although traditionally it is so thick you can almost eat it with a fork! This version is slightly more soup-like, and it's a great way to make the most of a glut of tomatoes.

1 kg ripe red tomatoes, preferably on the vine, chopped

300 ml vegetable stock (see page 26)

1 teaspoon caster sugar

6 tablespoons extra virgin olive oil

4 sprigs of oregano

4 sprigs of basil

125 g day-old bread, crusts removed

2 garlic cloves, halved

sea salt and freshly ground black pepper

freshly grated Parmesan cheese, to serve

**SERVES 4**

Put the tomatoes in a saucepan, add the stock, sugar, 2 tablespoons of the oil and the leaves from the oregano and most of the basil leaves, reserving a few for serving. Add a little salt and pepper, then heat slowly to boiling point. Reduce the heat, cover and simmer gently for 30 minutes.

Toast the bread, rub it all over with the garlic, then transfer to a plate. Sprinkle with the remaining oil and, using a fork, mash well into the bread, breaking it into small bits.

Add the bread to the soup and stir over a low heat for about 5 minutes until the bread has been evenly incorporated and the soup has thickened.

Add more salt and pepper to taste and serve hot, topped with a little grated Parmesan and the reserved basil leaves. This soup is also delicious served cold.

# watercress soup

Watercress has a fresh crunch that releases a subtle peppery taste – a real palate cleanser. Buy it in bunches, with long stems, an abundance of flawless dark green leaves and a clean fresh smell. It can only be stored in the fridge, wrapped in damp kitchen paper, for about 2 days, so make this soup with any leftovers.

Heat the oil in a large saucepan and add the onion, leek and potatoes. Cook for 15 minutes until soft and translucent. Add the flour, mix well, then add the stock and season with salt and pepper. Heat to simmering and cook for 30 minutes.

Using a hand-held blender, blend until smooth. Add the watercress and parsley and simmer for 5 minutes. Adjust the seasoning if necessary, then serve.

2 tablespoons olive oil

1 onion, chopped

1 leek, chopped

2 large potatoes, chopped

2 teaspoons plain flour

1.2 litres vegetable stock (see below)

300 g watercress, stalks removed and leaves chopped

a bunch of flat leaf parsley, chopped

sea salt and freshly ground black pepper

**SERVES 8**

# vegetable stock

Home-made stock, rather than that made from a stock cube, is better for making risotto or soup because it gives the best flavour. Make a stock with whatever fresh vegetables are available (the list on the right is just a suggestion), then refrigerate or freeze until needed.

Melt the butter and oil in a large, heavy saucepan. Add the garlic, sauté for 2 minutes, then add the remaining ingredients. Cook, stirring constantly, until softened but not browned.

Add 3 litres of water and bring to a boil. Reduce the heat, cover and simmer for 1½ hours. Let cool.

Return the pan to the heat and simmer for 15 minutes. Strain the stock and return to the pan. Discard the solids. Boil rapidly until reduced by half, then use as needed or let cool and keep in the fridge for up to 3 days.

40 g unsalted butter

1 tablespoon olive oil

3 garlic cloves, crushed

1 large onion, chopped

4 leeks, chopped

2 carrots, chopped

2 celery stalks, chopped

1 fennel bulb, chopped

a handful of fresh flat-leaf parsley, chopped

2 dried bay leaves

2 sprigs of thyme

**MAKES ABOUT 1 LITRE**

# white & green bean salad

3 tablespoons olive oil
1 tablespoon balsamic vinegar
800 g canned butter beans, drained and rinsed
300 g fine green beans, trimmed
100 g pumpkin seeds
sea salt and freshly ground black pepper

**SERVES 8**

The ingredients for this salad are very flexible: haricot beans or chickpeas could be used in place of the butter beans, and other green beans – such as mangetout, sugar snaps or sliced runner beans – in place of the fine green beans.

Put the oil and vinegar into a large serving bowl. Stir in the butter beans and set aside.

Cook the green beans in a saucepan of lightly salted boiling water for 3 minutes. Drain, refresh in several changes of cold water until cool, then drain again.

Add the green beans and pumpkin seeds to the serving bowl and stir well to mix everything together. Sprinkle with salt and pepper and serve.

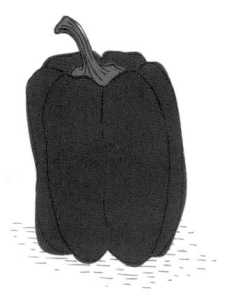

6 large tomatoes, halved

4 garlic cloves, thinly sliced

6 small aubergines,
thickly sliced lengthways

3 green or yellow courgettes,
thickly sliced lengthways

6 tablespoons olive oil, plus extra
for brushing

2 large red onions, thickly sliced

2 tablespoons chopped fresh
thyme leaves

sea salt and freshly ground
black pepper

sprigs of basil, to serve (optional)

### topping

grated zest of 1 unwaxed lemon

3 garlic cloves, crushed

about 140 g dried breadcrumbs

6 tablespoons freshly grated
Parmesan cheese

**SERVES 4–6**

# vegetable bake

Cook this tasty meal in a shallow dish for a wonderful
summer treat. Vegetables such as tomatoes and courgettes are
prone to lose a lot of liquid, so it's a good idea to remove
some beforehand by roasting or salting (this is known as
'degorging'). This is another useful dish to have in your
repertoire as you can vary the quantities of veg according
to what you have available.

Preheat the oven to 200°C (400°F) Gas 6.

Put the tomatoes on a baking sheet, cut side up, and push slivers
of garlic into each one. Roast in the preheated oven for about
30 minutes to remove some of the moisture.

Meanwhile, put the aubergines and courgettes on a plate, sprinkle
with salt and set aside for 30 minutes to extract some of the moisture.
Rinse and pat dry with kitchen paper.

Heat the oil in a large frying pan, add the onion and sauté until
softened and translucent. Remove from the pan and spread over
the base of a shallow ceramic ovenproof dish.

Arrange overlapping layers of the tomatoes, aubergines and
courgettes on top. Tuck the thyme between the layers and season
with pepper. Brush with the extra olive oil and bake in the oven
for 20 minutes.

Meanwhile, to make the topping, put the lemon zest and crushed
garlic in a bowl and mix well. Stir in the breadcrumbs and cheese,
then sprinkle over the top of the veg. Continue baking for at least
30 minutes or until browned, finishing under the grill if necessary.
Serve topped with basil leaves, if using.

# 3 wonderful carbs

## potatoes, rice & pasta

500 g white fish fillet such as
cod loin or haddock, or
salmon fillet

300 ml milk

a handful of fresh flat leaf
parsley sprigs

1 bay leaf

400 g mashed potato

1 tablespoon finely grated
unwaxed lemon zest

2 tablespoons chopped fresh
herbs, such as dill, parsley or
coriander

2–3 tablespoons wholemeal flour

2–3 tablespoons sunflower oil

sea salt and freshly ground
black pepper

## fish cakes

These fish cakes are packed with quality fish and are a brilliant way to turn leftover mashed potato into a tasty main course. If using fresh fish, make double quantities and freeze half after shaping. You can also grill or bake them in the oven until golden brown.

Rinse the fish and put it in a frying pan with the milk, parsley sprigs and bay leaf. Bring to the boil, then cover and simmer for about 10 minutes until the fish is cooked and the flesh looks white. Remove the fish with a slotted spoon and transfer it to a large bowl. Let it cool slightly and when cool enough to handle, remove the skin and any bones and flake the flesh. Discard the cooking liquor.

Add the mashed potato, lemon zest and chopped herbs to the fish. Season to taste with salt and pepper, then mix lightly. Using your hands, shape the mixture into 8 small fish cakes. Put the flour on a plate and coat the fish cakes in it. Transfer the fish cakes to a plate, cover lightly with clingfilm and chill in the refrigerator for at least 30 minutes.

To cook the fish cakes, heat the sunflower oil in a large frying pan. Add the fish cakes and cook for 4–5 minutes on each side until golden brown, crisp and piping hot. Serve immediately, with a green vegetable accompaniment.

# macaroni cheese with spinach

50 g butter
50 g plain flour
500 ml milk
300 g cooked macaroni, or
other pasta shapes
150 g cooked spinach, well drained
200 g Parmesan, freshly grated
sea salt and freshly ground
black pepper

SERVES 4

Pasta bakes, such as this recipe, are a great way to bring a new twist to leftover cooked pasta. Fresh or frozen spinach can be used in this recipe, but do make sure that both are thoroughly drained.

Preheat the oven to 190°C (375°F) Gas 5.

Melt the butter in a saucepan, remove from the heat and mix in the flour to make a roux. Return to a low heat and slowly pour in the milk, stirring constantly. Bring to the boil and cook for 1 minute, stirring frequently.

Add the macaroni to the sauce along with the spinach, seasoning and half the cheese. Mix well. Pour the mixture into an ovenproof dish, scatter the remaining cheese on top and bake in the preheated oven for 15 minutes, until golden.

# potato scones

Scottish cooks are famous around the world for their baking skills, and scones are perhaps their finest achievement. Mashed potato is used to replace some of the flour here, giving a light, moist texture and the cheese and ham give a delicious twist.

Preheat the oven to 220°C (425°F) Gas 7.

Heat a frying pan and dry-fry the ham or bacon for 5–6 minutes, or until crispy. Remove with a slotted spoon and leave to cool on kitchen paper.

Sift the flour, baking powder and salt together in a large bowl. Add the butter and rub in until the mixture resembles breadcrumbs.

Add the potato, cheese, oregano and cooked ham or bacon and mix well. Add enough milk to form a soft but firm dough, turn out onto a lightly floured work surface and knead briefly. Roll out the dough to 1.5 cm thick and, using a 6-cm biscuit cutter, stamp out rounds. Re-roll any trimmings and cut more rounds, to make about 10 in total.

Place the scones on a well-greased baking sheet, brush the tops with the beaten egg and bake for 10–15 minutes, or until golden brown and well risen. Leave to cool a little on a wire rack, then serve while still warm, spread with unsalted butter.

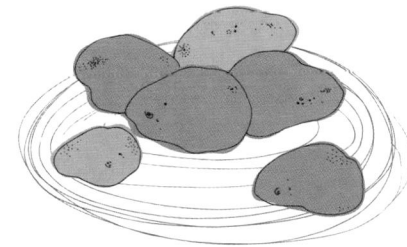

4 slices of ham or bacon, about 50 g, cut into small pieces

150–175 g plain flour

2 teaspoons baking powder

1/2 teaspoon salt

50 g unsalted butter, cubed

125 g cooked mashed potato

50 g hard cheese, cut into tiny cubes

1 teaspoon dried oregano

about 2 tablespoons milk

1 egg yolk, beaten, to glaze

**MAKES 10 SCONES**

# spicy fried potatoes & chorizo on toast

3 tablespoons olive oil

200 g boiled new potatoes, cut into bite-sized chunks

125 g chorizo sausage, cut into bite-sized chunks

1 garlic clove, crushed

$1/2$ teaspoon crushed dried chillies

4 slices of country-style sourdough bread

sea salt and freshly ground black pepper

**SERVES 2**

This recipe provides a great way to use leftover boiled new potatoes, and makes a really tasty brunch or lunch dish. Pancetta or bacon could be used instead of chorizo.

Heat the oil in a large frying pan until hot, then add the potatoes and fry for about 5 minutes. Add the chorizo and continue frying, turning occasionally, until the potatoes are crisp and golden. Sprinkle with the garlic and dried chillies and fry for a further 2 minutes.

Meanwhile, toast the bread on both sides. Spoon the potato and chorizo mixture on top, drizzling over any extra oil from the pan, then serve.

# cheesy mashed potato pie

This great accompaniment makes leftover mashed potato far more exciting – serve with roast chicken or pork and the meal is pretty much complete. Alternatively, this is useful when cooking for a mixed crowd of carnivores and vegetarians. Omit the ham and it can serve as a vegetarian main dish.

Preheat the oven to 190°C (375°F) Gas 5. Grease a baking dish or ceramic tart mould, 24 cm in diameter.

Heat the oil in a frying pan, add the onion and a pinch of salt and fry until browned, 5–7 minutes. Put the peas in a microwave-proof bowl with water to cover and microwave on high for 3 minutes, then drain. (Alternatively, blanch in boiling water for 3 minutes.)

Mix the mashed potato with the butter and milk or cream. Season with salt and stir in the egg until well blended.

Stir in the onion, peas, ham, chives and half the Cheddar. Season to taste. Transfer to the prepared dish and spread evenly. Sprinkle with the remaining Cheddar and bake in the preheated oven until well browned, 40–45 minutes. Serve hot or warm.

1 tablespoon extra virgin olive oil

1 onion, finely chopped

100 g shelled peas, fresh or frozen and thawed

1 kg mashed potato

30 g unsalted butter, softened

250 ml milk or cream (or a bit of both)

1 egg, beaten

50 g ham, sliced into thin ribbons (optional)

a small bunch of fresh chives, scissor-snipped

90 g mature Cheddar, grated

sea salt and freshly ground black pepper

**SERVES 4**

## rice balls

800 ml vegetable stock (see page 26)

50 g unsalted butter

275 g risotto rice, such as vialone nano, carnaroli or arborio

1 mozzarella cheese, about 125 g, cut into small cubes

6 shallots, finely chopped

handful of mixed fresh herbs, such as parsley, basil and oregano, chopped

finely grated zest of 1 large unwaxed orange

6 tablespoons freshly grated Parmesan cheese

6 tablespoons olive oil

sea salt and freshly ground black pepper

**breadcrumb coating**

1 egg, lightly beaten

50 g breadcrumbs (made from day-old bread)

**MAKES 8**

These cheesy rice balls, known as *supplì al telefono*, are enjoyed throughout Italy. In Sicily they are called *arancini*, meaning 'little oranges'. This is a good way of using risotto to make delicious party food or an antipasto. This recipe gives instructions for cooking the rice from scratch, but you can use rice leftover from last night's supper.

Put the stock in a saucepan. Heat until almost boiling, then reduce the heat until barely simmering to keep it hot.

Melt the butter in a wide saucepan. Add the rice and stir, using a wooden spoon, until the grains are well coated and glistening, about 1 minute. Add 1 ladle of hot stock and simmer, stirring until it has been absorbed.

Continue to add the stock at intervals and cook as before, until all the liquid has been absorbed and the rice is tender but still slightly firm – this will take about 18–20 minutes.

Add the mozzarella, shallots, herbs, zest, Parmesan, salt and pepper. Mix well. Remove from the heat and let cool. The rice is easier to shape when it is cold.

Using your hands, shape the flavoured rice into 8 balls. Dip each one into the beaten egg and coat well, then roll them in the breadcrumbs, pressing crumbs onto any uncovered area.

Heat the oil in a frying pan, add the rice balls (in batches, if necessary) and cook until golden on all sides, about 8 minutes. Drain well on kitchen paper. Serve hot or cold.

# rice & bean burgers

2 tablespoons Worcestershire sauce

1 onion, chopped

2 garlic cloves, crushed

200 g cooked brown rice (not quick-cook variety)

200 g tinned cannellini beans, drained and rinsed

200 g tinned red kidney beans, drained and rinsed

50 g wholemeal breadcrumbs (made from day-old bread)

1 egg, beaten

115 g mature Cheddar, grated

2 tablespoons freshly chopped thyme

1 small green pepper, deseeded and chopped

1 large carrot, coarsely grated

wholemeal flour or cornmeal, for coating

2–3 tablespoons sunflower oil

sea salt and freshly ground black pepper

**to serve**

salad leaves

relish

**MAKES 10–12**

There's something really satisfying about making your own burgers. These need to chill for 1½ hours so start them in advance. Pop any leftover burgers in the freezer before you cook them and take them out as and when you need them. This is a real 'use it up' recipe, combining cooked rice with breadcrumbs made from day-old bread and Cheddar cheese that has become too hard.

Put 2 tablespoons water and the Worcestershire sauce in a frying pan, add the onion and garlic and cook over medium heat until softened, about 8 minutes.

Put the onion, garlic, cooked rice, beans, breadcrumbs, egg, cheese and thyme in a food processor. Add plenty of seasoning, then process until combined. Add the green pepper and grated carrot and mix well. Refrigerate for 1½ hours, or until quite firm.

Shape the mixture into 10–12 burgers, using wet hands if the mixture sticks. Coat them in flour or cornmeal and chill for a further 30 minutes. Preheat the oven to 190°C (375°F) Gas 5.

Put the burgers on a non-stick baking sheet and brush lightly with a little oil. Cook in the preheated oven for 20–25 minutes, or until piping hot. Alternatively, heat the oil in a non-stick frying pan and fry the burgers for 3–4 minutes on each side, or until piping hot. Serve immediately with salad leaves and relish.

Variation: Add 1–2 deseeded finely chopped chillies to give an extra bite and 3 finely chopped celery sticks to add some crunch.

# chicken & tarragon pesto pasta

This really is a great dish for a quick summer lunch – tarragon and chicken are a match made in heaven. Kids will love it, yet it tastes good enough for adults to tuck into as well. Pesto can be made out of most herbs, so use whatever you have to hand and blend to create your own version. Any leftover pesto can be stored in the fridge for a couple of days.

To make the tarragon pesto, place the grated Parmesan, toasted pine nuts, tarragon, lemon zest and juice, garlic and olive oil in a jug and purée until smooth with a hand-held blender.

Put the cooked pasta, pesto, chicken and rocket in a serving bowl, season with salt and black pepper and toss well, coating the pasta and chicken evenly with the pesto. Serve immediately.

Variation: If you don't have any leftover cooked chicken, replace it with steamed summer vegetables such as courgettes, sugarsnap peas, broad beans or runner beans.

300 g cooked penne pasta
3 cooked chicken breasts, sliced
100 g rocket
sea salt and freshly ground black pepper

**tarragon pesto**

75 g Parmesan cheese, freshly grated
75 g pan-toasted pine nuts
a large bunch of tarragon, leaves stripped from the stem and chopped
grated zest and juice of 1 unwaxed lemon
1 garlic clove, crushed and chopped
5 tablespoons olive oil

**SERVES 4**

# spaghetti & rocket frittata

This is a great way to use up leftover spaghetti. The spaghetti is mixed with fresh arrabbiata sauce made with tomatoes and chillies to add a fiery kick.

3 tablespoons extra virgin olive oil

1 onion, chopped

1 garlic clove, crushed

3 ripe plum tomatoes, chopped

1 fresh red chilli, deseeded and finely chopped

2 tablespoons tomato purée

150 ml white wine or water

325 g cold cooked spaghetti (140 g before cooking)

6 large eggs

2 tablespoons freshly grated Parmesan

**to serve**

25 g rocket

2 tablespoons balsamic vinegar

sea salt and freshly ground black pepper

**SERVES 4**

Heat 1 tablespoon of the oil in a saucepan, add the onion and sauté for 5 minutes until softened. Add the garlic, tomatoes and chilli and cook for 3–4 minutes, stirring several times.

Add the tomato purée and wine or water and simmer for 5 minutes. Remove from the heat, add the cooked spaghetti and toss gently.

Break the eggs into a large bowl and whisk briefly with a fork. Add the spaghetti and sauce and mix gently.

Heat the remaining oil in a large, heavy-based non-stick frying pan, add the spaghetti and egg mixture and cook over a low heat for 10–12 minutes, or until golden brown on the underside and almost set on the top. Meanwhile, preheat the grill.

Sprinkle with the Parmesan and slide under the preheated grill for 30–60 seconds to melt the cheese and finish cooking the top. Leave to cool for 5 minutes, then transfer to a plate. Top with the rocket and sprinkle with balsamic vinegar.

# 4 make the most
# from a roast

# chilli beef noodles

100 g rice noodles
150 g cooked beef, thinly sliced
1 red onion, thinly sliced
2 garlic cloves, thinly sliced
1 red chilli, deseeded and thinly sliced
1 teaspoon sunflower oil
100 g beansprouts, rinsed
75 g mangetout, halved diagonally
1 tablespoon freshly squeezed lime juice
1 tablespoon Thai fish sauce
2 tablespoons chopped coriander,
to serve

**SERVES 2**

This is a dish of contrasts. It has a mixture of different textures in the soft noodles and crunchy vegetables, plus both hot and sour flavours.

Put the noodles in a heatproof bowl, cover with boiling water and let soak for 3 minutes. Drain and refresh with cold water, then set aside.

Toss the slices of beef together with the onion, garlic and chilli. Heat the sunflower oil in a non-stick frying pan or wok over high heat. Add the beef mixture and stir-fry for 2 minutes. Mix in the beansprouts and mangetout and cook, stirring, for 1 minute.

Stir the noodles into the pan with the lime juice and fish sauce and heat through. Pile into 2 serving bowls and serve immediately, topped with the chopped coriander.

# stir-fried chicken with greens

175 g green beans, halved
2 tablespoons peanut oil
5 cm fresh ginger, shredded
2 garlic cloves, sliced
250 g broccoli, broken into tiny florets
8 spring onions, halved crossways
1 red or yellow pepper, deseeded
and cut into strips
500 g cooked chicken,
cut into 5 cm strips or cubes
6 tablespoons chicken stock or water
2 tablespoons sweet chilli sauce
1 tablespoon light soy sauce
50 g mangetout (snowpeas), trimmed
50 g sugar snap peas, trimmed
100 g baby bok choy leaves, trimmed
noodles or rice, to serve

**SERVES 4**

There won't be many people who don't appreciate this dish. Stir-fried also effectively means 'steam-stirred', because the vegetables are mostly cooked in the aromatic steam. Use a sweet chilli sauce, not a fiery South-east Asian version.

To blanch the beans, bring a saucepan of water to the boil, add the beans and boil for 2–3 minutes until they turn bright green. Drain, run under cold water and drain again.

Put the oil in a wok and heat until very hot but not smoking. Alternatively, use a large, preferably non-stick, frying pan. Add the peanut oil, ginger and garlic and stir-fry for 2 minutes.

Add the broccoli, spring onions, green beans, sliced pepper, cooked chicken and chicken stock or water. Cover and cook for a further 2–3 minutes. Stir in the chilli sauce and soy sauce. Toss the mangetout, sugar snap peas and bok choy leaves on top. Cover and cook for 1–2 minutes.

Toss well and serve while the tastes and colours are still vivid and the textures crisp. Accompany with noodles or rice.

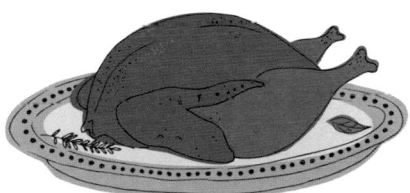

# quick couscous salad

This very quick and easy lunch dish is endlessly adaptable and is a great way to use up last night's leftover chicken. Easy-cook couscous is supposed to be just soaked then drained, but it's often better for a little more steaming or microwaving after soaking.

Put the couscous in a non-metal jug or bowl and cover with the stock or water. Leave for 15 minutes until the water has been absorbed. For a fluffier texture, put the soaked couscous in a strainer and steam over simmering water for another 10 minutes, or microwave in the jug or bowl on 50 per cent for about 5 minutes. Drain if necessary, pressing the liquid through the strainer with a spoon. Allow to cool.

When ready to make up the salad, put a layer of couscous in a lidded plastic container, then add a layer of chicken. Add the tomatoes, artichoke hearts, spring onions and chickpeas. Keep the leaves in a separate container until just before serving.

Put the oil in a screw-top jar, add the vinegar, mustard, if using, salt and pepper and mix well. Sprinkle over the salad. To serve, add the parsley and watercress and toss well.

4 tablespoons easy-cook wholegrain couscous

125 ml boiling chicken stock or water

1 cooked chicken breast, pulled into shreds

3 halves sun-blushed (semi-dried) tomatoes or 6 fresh cherry tomatoes, halved

2 marinated artichoke hearts, sliced

3–4 spring onions, sliced

400 g canned chickpeas, rinsed and drained

2–3 tablespoons extra virgin olive oil or 1 tablespoon pumpkin oil

1 teaspoon white rice vinegar or wine vinegar

1 teaspoon Dijon mustard (optional)

sea salt and freshly ground black pepper

a handful of flat leaf parsley, coarsely chopped, or a few sprigs of watercress

**SERVES 2**

100 g pine nuts

6 tablespoons extra virgin olive oil, preferably from Tuscany or Umbria

1 tablespoon wine vinegar, red or white

500 g roasted chicken

2 small red radicchio lettuces, leaves separated

4 tablespoons raisins

1–2 tablespoons balsamic vinegar

sea salt and freshly cracked black pepper

100 g fresh Parmesan cheese at room temperature, cut into shards, to serve

**SERVES 4**

# insalata gonzaga

This is a marvellously simple chicken salad named after the Gonzagas, who were the Dukes of Mantua, near Modena, the home of balsamic vinegar. True balsamic vinegar is rare and expensive, but use the best you can afford.

Put the pine nuts in a dry frying pan and heat, stirring, until lightly golden. Remove to a plate.

Put the oil and vinegar in a salad bowl, add a pinch of salt and beat with a fork. Slice the chicken or pull it into shreds. Add the chicken and radicchio to the bowl and toss gently.

Serve on salad plates, sprinkle with the raisins, pepper and balsamic vinegar and top with shards of Parmesan.

Note: If you wish, soak the raisins in verjuice for 10 minutes before adding to the salad. Verjuice is halfway between vinegar and wine – delicious, if a little difficult to find. Omit if necessary.

4 streaky bacon rashers

2 Hass avocados

1 large butterhead lettuce

6 ripe plum tomatoes,
cut into wedges

500 g cooked turkey, shredded,
at room temperature

2 hard-boiled eggs, quartered

100 g Roquefort cheese, cut into
thin slices, or crumbled

olive oil, for cooking

**lemon cream dressing**

250 ml double cream

freshly squeezed juice of 1 lemon

a handful of fresh chives,
scissor-snipped

**to serve**

crusty rolls

mini-cornichons, halved lengthways,
or sliced gherkins

**SERVES 4**

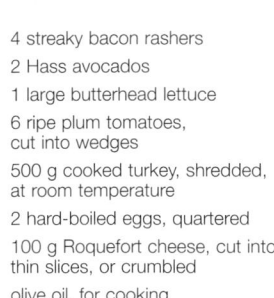

# turkey cobb salad

This American classic was invented in the Roaring Twenties by a Californian restaurateur named Cobb. It's essentially a 'bitser' salad – bitser this and bitser that – just like Niçoise or Gado Gado, two other legendary mixed salads. It's also a good post-turkey dish, when you have lots of turkey leftover and you're looking for an effortless way to serve it. Traditionally, the ingredients were arranged in lines but this version is jumbled together. The dressing is a lighter, fresher take on the customary mayonnaise.

Brush a frying pan with olive oil, add the bacon and cook until crispy but not crumbly. Remove and drain on crumpled kitchen paper.

Cut the avocados in half, remove the stones, then scoop out the flesh with a teaspoon.

Share the bacon, lettuce, tomatoes, turkey, eggs, cheese and avocado between 4 plates or bowls.

To make the dressing, put the cream in a bowl, add the lemon juice and beat well. Stir in the chives, then spoon over the salad and serve with crusty rolls and cornichons.

## chicken jalfrezi

3 tablespoons vegetable oil

1 onion, roughly chopped

2 garlic cloves, crushed

1 tablespoon Madras curry paste

1 tablespoon tomato purée

400 g canned chopped tomatoes (flavoured with mixed herbs, if available)

1 teaspoon red wine vinegar

125 g chargrilled red peppers, chopped

125 g courgettes, diced

450 g cooked chicken, cut into bite-sized pieces

sea salt and freshly ground black pepper

coriander sprigs, to garnish

**SERVES 6**

You can make this tantalizingly spicy chicken jalfrezi in less time than you might wait for a takeaway delivery. Use a jar of prepared chargrilled peppers and look out for good-quality curry pastes in supermarkets. Go for a hot variety containing spices such as chilli, cumin, coriander, tamarind and turmeric. Serve with jasmine rice and ready-cooked poppadoms.

Heat the oil in a large frying pan, reduce the heat and add the onion and garlic. Saute over medium heat until golden. Add the curry paste and cook for 1 minute to cook off the spices.

Add the tomato purée, chopped tomatoes, vinegar and 200 ml water to the frying pan. Bring to the boil and simmer, uncovered, for 5 minutes.

Add the chargrilled red peppers and diced courgettes to the pan and cook for a further 5 minutes until the courgettes are tender. Stir in the chicken pieces and season with salt and pepper. Simmer gently for another 6–7 minutes, or until the chicken is piping hot.

Just before serving, garnish with coriander sprigs. Great served with jasmine rice and poppadoms.

# chilli con carne

2 tablespoons corn oil or beef dripping

2 onions, sliced

3 garlic cloves, sliced

500 g roast beef, cut into 1.5 cm cubes

2 tablespoons plain flour

410 g canned red kidney beans, drained and rinsed

2 tablespoons tomato paste

$^1/_4$–$^1/_2$ tablespoon chilli powder, dried chilli flakes, or 1–4 whole red serrano chillies, deseeded if preferred, and chopped

1 green pepper, deseeded and chopped

$^1/_4$ teaspoon ground cumin

1 litre beef stock

salt, to taste

**SERVES 4**

This Texan classic is almost always made with chilli powder, but it is also good made with crushed dried chillies or sliced fresh ones – adjust the quantity of chilli to suit your tastebuds. This speedy variation replaces minced beef with leftover roast beef, and dried kidney beans with tinned.

Put the oil or dripping in a large frying pan and heat until melted. Add the onion and garlic and cook gently until softened and lightly browned, about 15 minutes. Transfer to a plate and keep warm.

Add the beef to the pan, stir in the flour and mix well. Add the drained kidney beans, tomato paste, chilli, green pepper, cumin and beef stock. Bring to the boil, transfer to a casserole or saucepan, cover with a lid and simmer on top of the stove for 30 minutes. If the mixture needs to thicken up, remove the lid and turn up the heat to reduce the liquid.

To serve, ladle the chilli con carne into warmed serving bowls. If you wish, sprinkle with chopped coriander and top with a spoonful of sour cream. Serve with warmed tortillas or rice, or use as a topping for a baked potato.

If you wish to stretch the leftover beef to serve more people, simply add an additional can of drained kidney beans and another chopped pepper (either green or red).

3 tablespoons butter
1 onion, diced
1 garlic clove, finely chopped
300 g roast beef, diced
700 g roast or boiled potatoes, diced
½ teaspoon Tabasco Sauce
1 tablespoon pure vegetable oil
4 eggs
salt and freshly ground black pepper

**SERVES 4**

# corned beef hash

The British invented bubble and squeak to use up leftovers from a dinner of beef brisket, potato and cabbage. Americans dropped the cabbage and called it corned beef hash. This adaptation is a mixture of the two recipes and uses leftover roast beef, rather than the more American corned beef brisket, but it still tastes just as good and makes a great brunch dish.

Heat 1 tablespoon of the butter in a large, heavy frying pan. Add the onion, garlic and beef. Season and sauté for 5 minutes. Pour the mixture into a bowl with the potatoes. Add the Tabasco and mix together well.

Add the remaining butter to the frying pan. Pour the potato mixture into it and press everything down firmly. Cover with a heavy lid or plate that will fit just inside the pan to weigh the mixture down. Cook over a medium heat for 10 minutes. Turn the mixture over in batches and cook for 10 minutes on the other side. The meat should be brown and crisp; keep cooking and turning if it isn't.

Make 4 indentations in the potatoes and crack an egg into each. Place a fitted lid over the pan and cook until the eggs are done. Alternatively, in a separate non-stick frying pan, heat 1 tablespoon vegetable oil and fry the eggs. Place one fried egg on top of each serving of corned beef hash. You can also poach the eggs instead of frying them.

# classic tomato sauce with beef

The traditional way to eat this would be to serve the sauce with the pasta and to follow with the beef, a selection of salads and some crusty bread, but here the beef is cut into slices and mixed with the pasta and sauce.

Put the herbs, garlic, semi-dried or sun-dried tomatoes and capers into a food processor and process until finely chopped. Put the beef slices flat onto a work surface and sprinkle lightly with salt and freshly ground black pepper. Spread the herb mixture evenly over each slice and roll up tightly, tying string around the middle to secure.

Heat the olive oil until very hot in a large sauté pan, add the rolled beef and cook for 1–2 minutes until browned all over. Add the canned tomatoes and salt and pepper to taste. Cook for 20 minutes until the sauce is thickened and pulpy.

Meanwhile, bring a large saucepan of water to the boil. Add a good pinch of salt, then the pasta, and cook until al dente, or according to the timings on the packet.

Transfer the beef from the sauce to a chopping board. Remove and discard the string, then cut each slice of beef crossways into chunky slices.

Drain the pasta and return it to the warm pan. Add the sauce and beef to the pasta and toss to mix. Divide between 4 bowls, top with parsley and serve.

1 tablespoon chopped fresh rosemary

2 tablespoons chopped fresh flat leaf parsley, plus extra to serve

2 garlic cloves, crushed

4 semi-dried sunblush tomatoes, or sun-dried tomatoes

2 teaspoons salted capers, rinsed well

400g roast beef, thickly sliced

1 tablespoon olive oil

800 g canned plum tomatoes

300 g dried pasta, such as conchiglie or rigatoni

salt and freshly ground black pepper

**SERVES 4**

# lamb navarin

This adaptation of a classic recipe allows you to create a great new dish from yesterday's roast lamb. The vegetables added towards the end of the cooking time can either be freshly cooked, or leftovers from the previous day. To give the gravy that rich colour and sweet flavour, a little sugar is sprinkled into the pan. It is then caramelized: the darker the sugar becomes, the less sweet the stew will be.

Preheat the oven to 190°C (375°F) Gas 5.

Melt the butter in a frying pan. Sprinkle over the sugar and let it caramelize to a deep golden brown. (Be careful not to caramelize it too much, as it burns easily.) Quickly mix in the flour, add the cubed lamb and mix well: this will let the flour cook a little.

Add the stock, then the tomatoes, garlic and herbs. Stir gently and bring to a boil. Season to taste, then transfer to a lidded casserole, cover and simmer in the oven for 30 minutes.

If there is too much liquid, strain it off into a saucepan, bring to a boil, and simmer until reduced to about 600 ml. Taste and adjust the seasoning, then add the cooked vegetables. Mix them gently through the liquid, then transfer them and the liquid to the casserole, stir gently, then reheat in the oven for about 10 minutes before serving.

3 tablespoons butter

1 tablespoon sugar

2 tablespoons plain flour

1 kg cooked lamb, cut into 2.5-cm cubes

600 ml lamb or beef stock

4 tomatoes, peeled and deseeded, or 200 g canned Italian plum tomatoes

2 garlic cloves, crushed

1 teaspoon chopped fresh thyme leaves

1 sprig of rosemary

1 bay leaf

salt and freshly ground black pepper

### spring vegetables

8 new potatoes, scraped and cooked

8 baby carrots, scraped and cooked

8 baby white turnips, cooked

125 g green peas, cooked

125 g green beans, cooked and cut into 1 cm strips

**SERVES 4**

# 5 yesterday's bread

## french onion soup

50 g unsalted butter

1 tablespoon extra virgin olive oil

3 large onions, about 1.3 kg, thinly sliced

2 garlic cloves, crushed

1 tablespoon plain flour

1 litre beef or chicken stock

600 ml dry white wine

1 fresh bay leaf

2 sprigs of thyme

1 baguette, or other white bread, sliced

about 180 g freshly grated Gruyère cheese

coarse salt and freshly ground black pepper

**SERVES 4–6**

Synonymous with bistro eating, this simplified version of a classic recipe is the ideal dish when all your kitchen cupboard contains is just a few onions, a slightly stale loaf of bread and cheese that has gone a little hard.

Put the butter and oil in a large saucepan and melt over medium heat. Add the onions and cook over a low heat until soft, 15–20 minutes.

Add the garlic and flour and cook, stirring for about 1 minute. Add the stock, wine, bay leaf and thyme. Season with salt and pepper and bring to the boil. Boil for 1 minute, then lower the heat and simmer very gently for 20 minutes. Taste and adjust the seasoning with salt and pepper. At this point, the soup will be cooked, but standing time will improve the flavour – at least 30 minutes.

Before serving, preheat the grill. Put the baguette slices on a baking tray and brown under the grill until lightly toasted. Set aside.

To serve, ladle the soup into ovenproof bowls and top with a few toasted baguette rounds. Sprinkle grated cheese over the top and cook under the grill until browned and bubbling. Serve immediately.

2 eggs
2 thick slices of white bread
6 slices of bacon
1 tablespoon olive oil
2 large tomatoes, halved lengthways
1 teaspoon sugar
10 g butter
a few basil leaves, torn (optional)
sea salt and freshly ground black pepper

**SERVES 2**

# eggy bread
## with bacon & tomatoes

This recipe is actually best made with bread that's a day old as it will soak up more of the eggy mixture and fry better than fresh bread. This is the perfect dish for Saturday morning breakfast, when you need to use up ingredients before doing the weekly food shop.

Put the eggs in a bowl and beat until blended. Season well. Pour into a shallow bowl, then dip the slices of bread, turning them over so that they are well coated in the beaten egg. Leave to stand for a few minutes so the bread really absorbs the egg.

Meanwhile, grill or fry the bacon until crisp. Transfer to a low oven to keep it warm.

Heat half the olive oil in a frying pan until hot. Add the tomatoes and sprinkle with the sugar. Fry for 1–2 minutes on each side until caramelized. Transfer to a plate and put in the oven with the bacon to keep warm.

Wipe the frying pan clean with kitchen paper, add the butter and remaining oil and heat until hot. Add the egg-soaked slices of bread, fry for 1 minute, then turn over and fry for a further minute until crisp and golden on both sides.

Place the French toast on warmed plates, top with the bacon and tomatoes, then sprinkle with the basil, if using, and serve immediately.

# sardine bruschetta

This Italian-inspired toasted sandwich is extremely versatile and makes a deliciously quick brunch or lunch dish. Slightly stale bread works well here – anything too fresh will collapse under the weight of the topping.

120 g tinned sardines
1 teaspoon balsamic vinegar
1 slice of wholemeal bread, lightly toasted
1 tablespoon finely grated Cheddar cheese (optional)
3–4 cherry tomatoes, halved

**SERVES 1**

Preheat the grill to medium.

Put the sardines and balsamic vinegar in a bowl and mash with a fork. Pile the sardines on top of the toasted bread and sprinkle with the grated cheese, if using.

Transfer to a grill rack with the tomatoes and cook under the preheated grill for 2–3 minutes, or until the cheese is golden brown and the tomatoes are hot.

Put the tomatoes on top of the toast and cut it into fingers.

# italian bread salad

This Tuscan salad, best made with day-old bread, is the perfect way to use up leftovers. It is highly flexible so use whatever ingredients you have to hand – sourdough bread, a little garlic, a bunch of basil.

Put the bread cubes in a large bowl with the tomato, cucumber, onion and chopped parsley.

Add the olives, capers, olive oil, vinegar, lemon juice, sugar, salt and pepper, then mix well.

Leave the salad to stand for 1 hour before serving so that the bread soaks up the juices and all the flavours mingle.

4 slices country bread, cubed

4 ripe tomatoes, cut into wedges

15 cm cucumber, peeled and cut into chunks

1 red onion, sliced

a bunch of flat leaf parsley, coarsely chopped

100 g olives, pitted

50 g capers

4 tablespoons olive oil

1 1/2 tablespoons wine vinegar

freshly squeezed juice of 1/2 lemon

1 teaspoon caster sugar

salt and freshly ground black pepper

**SERVES 4**

# orange cream panettone

Panettone is a sweet yeast bread traditionally eaten at Christmas in Italy. However, there always seems to be some leftover by the time New Year comes around, so try this recipe. Somewhere between a light and fluffy bread-and-butter pudding and a squidgy French toast, this is a divine concoction.

To make the orange cream, mix together the crème fraîche, icing sugar, lemon juice and orange juice until smooth and creamy. Set aside.

Put the egg yolks, cream, orange zest, juice and sugar in a wide, shallow dish and beat well. Heat the butter in a large non-stick frying pan. Dip each slice of panettone in the eggy mixture, turning over so that each side is coated, then place in the frying pan. Spoon any remaining eggy mixture over the panettone and fry for 2 minutes, or until golden underneath.

Very carefully flip the toasts over and cook for a further 1–2 minutes until golden. Place the French toast on warmed plates. Dust with icing sugar, spoon over the orange cream and decorate with orange zest. Eat immediately.

2 large egg yolks
00 ml single cream
freshly grated zest of ¹/₂ orange
2 teaspoons freshly squeezed orange juice
1 teaspoon sugar
15 g unsalted butter
2 thick slices of panettone, cut in half
icing sugar, to dust
strips of orange zest, to decorate

### orange cream

3 tablespoons crème fraîche
1 teaspoon icing sugar
¹/₂ teaspoon lemon juice
1 tablespoon orange juice

**SERVES 2**

# bread & butter puddings

Bread and butter pudding is classic comfort food. This version updates a wonderfully retro recipe, using tea cakes or hot cross buns – these are great eaten fresh on the day they have been baked, but they do go stale quickly.

Preheat the oven to 180°C (350°F) Gas 4. Generously butter six 200-ml ramekins.

Put the milk, cream, vanilla extract and 3 tablespoons of the sugar into a saucepan and heat until the sugar dissolves.

Put the eggs into a bowl, whisk well, stir in 2–3 tablespoons of the hot milk mixture just to warm the eggs, then stir in the remainder of the hot milk.

Lightly toast the tea cakes or hot cross buns and cut them into quarters. Divide the pieces between the 6 prepared ramekins and sprinkle with the sultanas. Pour in the custard mixture, grate a little nutmeg over the top and sprinkle with the remaining sugar.

Bake in the preheated oven for 18–20 minutes until firm. Let cool a little, then serve warm with cream, if liked.

300 ml milk

300 ml double cream

½ teaspoon vanilla extract

4 tablespoons caster sugar

3 eggs

6 tea cakes or hot cross buns, halved

50 g sultanas

freshly grated nutmeg, to taste

pouring cream, to serve (optional)

**SERVES 6**

# croissant pudding

This is another version of bread and butter pudding, using aged croissants. Chocolate croissants, brioche and even panettone will do. Embellish the recipe with chocolate chips, rum-soaked raisins or spoons of fruit conserve.

Preheat the oven to 180°C (350°F) Gas 4. Generously butter a baking dish.

Cut each croissant into 3 and arrange the pieces in the prepared baking dish. Put the eggs in a mixing bowl and beat well.

Put the milk, crème fraîche and sugar in a measuring jug and whisk well. Pour into the beaten eggs and whisk again, then pour the mixture over the croissants. Sprinkle the top of the pudding liberally with sugar.

Bake in the preheated oven until golden and the batter is just set, 30–40 minutes. Serve warm.

4 all-butter croissants, preferably stale (but not too stale)

3 large eggs

300 ml whole milk

3 heaped tablespoons crème fraîche or double cream

50 g sugar, plus extra for sprinkling

**SERVES 4**

# sticky fried bananas
## on toast

One mouthful of these buttery, sticky, gooey, tangy bananas will transport you to another world – just be careful about putting too much in your mouth in one go because those bananas are so hot when they first come out of the pan! Challah, the delicious, dense Jewish bread, makes the perfect base, but any good-quality white bread will be divine.

50 g butter, plus extra for spreading

3 very ripe bananas, sliced

2 tablespoons brown sugar

1 tablespoon brandy

juice of ¹/₂ lime

2 thick slices of challah or white bread

thick cream or vanilla ice cream, to serve

**SERVES 2**

Melt the butter in a non-stick pan until sizzling, then add the bananas and fry for about 2 minutes. Turn them over, sprinkle with the brown sugar and continue cooking for a further 2–3 minutes, gently nudging the bananas around the pan, but take care not to break them up.

Add the brandy and cook for 1 minute more until the bananas are soft and tender, letting the juices bubble. Remove the pan from the heat, squeeze over the lime juice and jiggle the bananas to mix.

Meanwhile, lightly toast the bread on both sides, add the bananas and pour over thick cream or top with a generous scoop of vanilla ice cream. Serve immediately.

# banana bread

This recipe is ideal for using up very ripe bananas – in fact, the riper and softer they are, the better. Slices of banana bread make a great addition to lunchboxes, or serve for afternoon tea.

100g butter or baking margarine, softened

225 g sugar

2 eggs

3 very ripe bananas

1 teaspoon lemon juice

225 g self-raising flour

¹/₂ teaspoon ground nutmeg

Preheat the oven to 180°C (350°F) Gas 4. Line a 900-g loaf tin with baking paper.

Cream the butter or margarine and sugar together in a large mixing bowl, using a wooden spoon. Stir in the eggs.

Using a fork, mash the bananas on a plate and stir in the lemon juice. Tip the mashed bananas into the creamed butter and sugar, then sift in the flour and nutmeg. Mix thoroughly.

Pour the cake batter into the prepared tin. Bake for 1–1¼ hours, or until a skewer inserted into the centre of the cake comes out clean. Allow to cool in the tin for 10 minutes, then transfer to a wire cooling rack. Store in an airtight container.

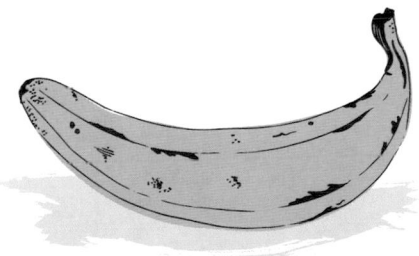

3 large cooking apples, peeled,
quartered, cored and sliced

3–4 tablespoons caster sugar

250 g fresh or frozen raspberries

vanilla ice cream or
pouring cream, to serve

**crumble topping**

150 g plain flour

25 g ground almonds

110 g butter,
chilled and cubed

50 g caster sugar

25 g flaked almonds (optional)

**SERVES 6**

# raspberry, apple & almond crumble

The addition of raspberries to this otherwise traditional crumble
not only gives it a gorgeous colour but creates a pleasing tartness. Crumbles
are a great way to use up fruit, so experiment with different combinations:
apple and blackberry, pear and raspberry, or whatever you fancy.

Put the apples in a large saucepan. Sprinkle over 3 tablespoons sugar and add
3 tablespoons water. Cover the pan, place over a low heat and cook for about 15
minutes, shaking the pan occasionally until the apple pieces are soft but still holding
their shape. Stir in the raspberries and check for sweetness, adding a little extra sugar
if it seems too sharp. Transfer to a lightly greased shallow ovenproof dish and let cool.

To make the topping, put the flour and ground almonds in a large bowl. Keep
cutting the butter cubes into the flour mixture until you can't get the
pieces of butter any smaller, then rub the butter and flour
mixture together using your fingertips, until the mixture
resembles coarse breadcrumbs. Stir in the sugar and rub
for another minute. Stir in the flaked almonds, if using.

When the fruit has cooled, preheat the oven to 200°C
(400°F) Gas 6.

Spread the crumble mixture evenly over the fruit,
making sure you cover the whole surface. Bake in the
preheated oven for about 35–40 minutes until the
topping is golden and the fruit juices are bubbling
around the sides of the dish. Leave to cool for 10–15
minutes before serving.

# red berry smoothie

Even people with a dairy intolerance are
often able to eat yoghurt, since it changes
its structure during fermentation, so this
is a lovely, satisfying drink to fill you up for
the morning, and a great way to use up any
leftover berries in the fruit bowl.

about 250 g berries, such as
strawberries, cranberries,
redcurrants or raspberries (for a pink
smoothie), or blackberries and
blueberries (for a blue smoothie)

250 ml natural yoghurt

125 ml crushed ice

sugar or honey, to taste

**SERVES 2–3**

Put all the ingredients into
a blender and work to a thin,
frothy cream. If your blender
doesn't crush ice, add it at the
end. If the smoothie is too
thick, add a little water and
blend again. Taste, then add
sugar or honey if you prefer.

# helpful hints & tasty tips

Here are some more ideas for making the most of your leftovers.

✱ When reheating leftovers, always make sure they are piping hot.

✱ Rather than throwing away stale bread, make breadcrumbs for use in stuffings or bread sauce, or to top gratins. Discard the crusts, cut the bread into cubes and whizz in a food processor, then freeze until required.

✱ To freshen up a day-old loaf, hold it for just a second or two under a running cold tap. Give it a good shake and place it in a hot oven for about 10 minutes; it will come out as soft and crusty as freshly baked bread.

✱ Stale bread also makes great croûtons to serve with soup or to toss in a green salad. Cut the bread into cubes and shallow-fry in a frying pan until golden on all sides. Drain on kitchen paper.

✱ Don't discard dry end-pieces of cheese. Grate them and freeze in a zipper-style freezer bag. Use in any recipe that requires a sprinkling of grated cheese on top before cooking or baking.

✱ If you have half a jar of leftover pesto, mix it with softened butter and freeze in individual portions. Use the pesto butter on steaks and grilled chicken.

✱ Leftover pasta makes a great lunch the next day. Mix with mayonnaise or salad dressing and add chopped veg, such as tomatoes and spring onions, grated courgette or drained sweetcorn. You can also use up leftover rice in the same way.

✱ As well as using up leftover roast meat in the recipes given in this book, you can slice and freeze it, to use at a later date in a curry.

✱ Any leftover spaghetti can be added to a stir-fry to turn it into chow mein.

✱ Leftover boiled potatoes can be thinly sliced and added to omelettes, or chopped, then mixed with mayonnaise and snipped chives to make a tasty potato salad.

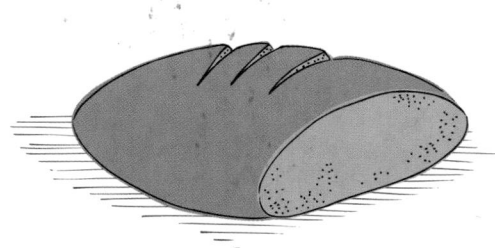

## store-cupboard standbys

Having a well-stocked store cupboard or pantry will help you to stretch leftovers into a tasty meal.

✱ Leftover salsa makes a great pizza topping – spread over the pizza base and add toppings of your choice. Or stir it into a chilli or add it to a pasta sauce.

✱ If you are left with half a lemon or lime, squeeze the juice into ice-cube trays and freeze for later use.

✱ Grate leftover Cheddar cheese into mashed potato to add extra flavour.

✱ If using a breadmaker, add stale or leftover cereal crumbs to the mixture (reduce the quantity of flour accordingly).

✱ Leftover wine can be frozen in ice cube trays to add to gravies, stews and casseroles.

✱ To stretch leftover soup, add some more stock and, if you have it, some cream to help thicken it.

✱ Keep your store cupboard stocked up with ingredients such as spices, dried herbs and sauces to add extra flavour to your leftovers.

✱ Tinned chopped tomatoes and cartons of passata are useful for making instant pasta sauces. Chop up leftover veg, such as onions, mushrooms and red peppers, cook gently in a little oil, then pour over the tomatoes for a quick and easy sauce.

✱ Tinned kidney beans, cannellini beans, lentils and chickpeas are useful for stretching leftovers, particularly casseroles, and adding bulk to a dish.

✱ Keep a good stock of dried pasta in different shapes – it's perfect for mixing with leftover roast meat and turning into a pasta bake.

✱ Rice is the perfect accompaniment to stir-fries, which are a great way to make the most of leftover vegetables. You can even add in strips of cooked chicken or beef left from the Sunday roast.

# index

# recipe credits

The recipes in this book are adapted from original recipes by:

**Fiona Beckitt**
Raspberry, apple & almond crumble

**Susannah Blake**
Cheese scones
Orange cream pannetone
Spicy fried potatoes & chorizo on toast
Sticky fried bananas on toast

**Celia Brooks Brown**
American pancakes
Rarebit

**Tamsin Burnett-Hall**
Chilli beef noodles

**Clare Ferguson**
Roasted vegetables
Stir-fried chicken with greens

**Ursula Ferrigno**
Rice balls
Vegetable stock

**Silvana Franco**
Carbonara
Cheese pasta bake
Classic tomato sauce with beef

**Gillian Haslam**
Banana bread
Eggy bread with bacon and tomatoes

**Rachael Anne Hill**
Fish cakes
Rice and bean burgers
Sardine bruschetta

**Jennifer Joyce**
Corned beef hash

**Caroline Marson**
Chicken jalfrezi

**Anna Nichols**
Potato scones

**Elsa Petersen-Schepelern**
Grilled courgettes
Insalata gonzaga
Pumpkin risotto
Quick couscous salad
Red berry smoothie
Tomato and bean soup
Turkey Cobb salad

**Louise Pickford**
Bread & butter pudding
Meringues
Pappa al pomodoro

**Jennie Shapter**
Hearty country-style tortilla
Pepper omelette
Spaghetti & rocket frittata

**Sonia Stevenson**
Chilli con carne
Lamb navarin
Vegetable bake

**Laura Washburn**
Cauliflower cheese
Croissant pudding
French onion soup
Mashed potato pie
Yoghurt cake

**Fran Warde**
Carrot and spinach mash
Chicken and tarragon pesto pasta
Chickpea and vegetable curry
Italian bread salad
Macaroni cheese with spinach
Watercress soup
White and green bean salad

# photographs

Peter Cassidy
Pages 18, 42, 43, 44, 45, 53, 54, 57, 61

William Lingwood
Pages 11, 29, 46, 48, 49, 55, 58

Martin Brigdale
Pages 10, 12, 22, 23, 47, 50

Debi Treloar
Pages 16, 21, 24, 27, 38

Tara Fisher
Pages 6, 19, 39

Ian Wallace
Pages 15, 25

Philip Webb
Pages 9, 13

Caroline Arber
Pages 32

Nicki Dowey
Pages 37

Jason Lowe
Pages 36

David Munns
Pages 35

Noel Murphy
Page 30

Peter Myers
Pages 33

Craig Robertson
Page 29

William Reavell
Pages 40